THANK YOU FOR

BEST W_____   MIKE !

MW01118364

Dare to Lead

NiCK,
NEVER FORGET THE
6 MAGIC WORDS

Nick —
Wishing you all the
success in the world.
— Stephen

Nick,
My Funny Man!
Thank you for making
us laugh during our
training. Good Luck
— Melissa

Nick —
Your determination
is inspiring.

Dare to Lead

✦

Leading with Respect, Sincerity, and Service

Thomas A. Lutz

iUniverse, Inc.
New York Lincoln Shanghai

Dare to Lead
Leading with Respect, Sincerity, and Service

iUniverse, Inc.

For information address:
iUniverse, Inc.
2021 Pine Lake Road, Suite 100
Lincoln, NE 68512
www.iuniverse.com

ISBN: 0-595-30901-1

Printed in the United States of America

This book is dedicated to my wife Aleene and our family (son Jeff, the weather forecaster; daughter Amy, her husband Brendon and their son Truman). Together they encouraged me to write and then coerced me to complete this work. During the fall of 2003, Aleene and I were able to spend time visiting family from Virginia to Oregon. We spent a lot of quiet time together while on the road. She listened to my ideas, helped me refine them, and kept me on course by reminding me that I had to get this project completed and use it as a springboard in my new career as consultant and mediator. She gave me reflective advice and time alone to get it done. The kids served as an inspiration. Visits to the coast of Oregon and the north woods of Michigan inspired me to write and think clearly.

Encouragement is much more of a motivator for me than is fear or intimidation. Keeping that in mind, Aleene would remind me of how great I would feel when this task was completed. Of course, she was right. It was an exciting project that they all contributed to.

Contents

Foreword

Leadership is a subject that elicits opinions from everyone who has served as a leader (whether formally or informally) and from everyone who has ever been led. When it comes to defining leadership, we Americans are like the judge who made this observation about the definition of pornography, "…I know it when I see it." Good leadership is like that…we know it when we experience it. Unfortunately, going into the workplace and being asked—or appointed—to lead a group of employees without some idea of how to behave in an appropriate leadership manner is full of risks.

Managing things and people, scheduling the flow of work, or directing individuals to accomplish tasks is not leadership. The classic definition of leadership is "Achieving the goals of the organization through people." While that gets closer to the truth, effective leadership involves developing a personal bond between the leader and his charges that allows good things to happen. Good things, of course, mean productive, value-added activities that achieve the goals of the organization without the fallout of turnover, unresolved conflict and the like.

Leadership is often intrinsic. There are technical components which can be learned in a seminar or read about; then there are the practical pieces of the puzzle that can only be experienced. For example, a cookbook is a technical approach to food preparation. Being a great cook combines the ability to blend the correct ingredients in the right amounts with the right timing and coordination necessary to prepare a savory dish. Good leadership is like that.

This book is intended to shorten the experience gap. It is not a cookbook. It is intended to be a practical guide with some personal examples sprinkled in to help the new leader (or the less experienced older one) to develop strong bonds with his charges. There are no shortcuts. The ability to recognize signs of good leadership along the way will make the journey more pleasurable for everyone. Hopefully, as you read this book you will pick up some cues to improve your leadership skills.

Introduction

The woman's voice on the phone made her problem sound ominous; it was low and serious. She wanted to talk to me face-to-face, but she didn't want to be seen coming to my office. We set up a meeting off campus and after hours. She was a relatively new manager in an administrative department of the hospital where I was human resources director. Her staff was made up of approximately ten well-educated women. She simply stated that she had an employee problem that she wanted to discuss.

When I arrived at our meeting, Margaret avoided the serious nature of our phone conversation for a few minutes, then she told me why she asked me to meet her in such a clandestine manner. One of her employees was threatening her authority by acting out behavior which included eye-rolling, heavy sighing, and challenging comments at the mention of some issues. These behaviors came out in front of colleagues during staff meetings. Her question was simple: "What can I do?" The discussion that followed was about an hour and a half of Supervisor 101 on leadership, discipline, performance management and related topics.

That afternoon I told Margaret that leading people—whether into battle, literally, or into the battles of the workplace—is hard work. Leadership requires that we (1) take action and (2) have patience so we can become respected and enthusiastically followed by those being led. The leader does not have to be a tyrant, but the leader cannot be a friend, either. Margaret was "one of them" less than two years before. Today she was in charge. She was struggling with her role as the boss. She didn't want to offend her nemesis, but she knew it was time to take action. She could feel her power slipping away. She was looking for guidance.

Margaret told me that she and her husband had successfully reared a teenage daughter. She said that while she thought she knew about bizarre behavior from that experience, she added that she was not too proud to ask for help with one of her highly intelligent, but misguided employees. "I never knew things like this could happen in the workplace," she said.

As I drove back to my office, my mind traced over the 90-minute conversation. I blurted out loud, "I should write a book about this stuff." The days passed and I continued to think about all the reasons and all the people and all the situations that could be included in such a work. The ideas had all been in my mind previously. What this meeting changed was the evidence of compelling need. New managers need leadership information to be able to take positive action, but they often lack the knowledge of how to proceed. They often don't ask for help. Either they think they are very sophisticated and don't want to ask questions, they think they know the answers already, or they are too embarrassed to ask for assistance, all of which are wrong reflexes to a leadership dilemma.

Leaders do the things necessary through human interaction to achieve the goals of the organization. Great leaders soften the hard rules of leadership by using their interpersonal skills that allow for a current of energy to flow from leader to those being led. The overlying motivation changes from power to compassion. There is a difference between a decisive leader and a tyrant, however. The leadership gift is to be able to distinguish between the two and act appropriately.

A commanding officer of mine, Jerry Miller, captain of an aircraft carrier I was serving in, told a group of us junior officers at a leadership meeting that "A good ship is a happy ship." I came to discover that Captain Miller knew what he was talking about. He took command of a relatively old ship, just out of the shipyard after a long overhaul period, which meant that much of the crew (including the leadership) had changed. He molded the new sailors and officers into a highly trained, fighting unit. Over a period of about six months, he developed the Franklin D. Roosevelt into a "Happy Ship." That was a long time ago. Over the years I often wondered, "Do the lessons learned in the 1960s still apply in the modern age?" My experience has been that they do.

The meaning of "happy," as Captain Miller used the term, is what all leaders try to establish as they struggle to keep any organization of human beings in balance. It is the connection that is made between leader and followers that determines whether working together is a pleasant, or at least a tolerable process, or not. There are two ends of this continuum: One is being a bully and the other is being a pushover. Neither approach works over the long haul. The middle ground is where the best work gets done. "Happy" did not mean that the sailors were getting enough food, rest, mail, and liberty. It meant that they would do whatever job they were asked because a bond was established between those in charge and the crew—between the skipper and his men.

Some leaders understand this dynamic early in their careers, and some never seem to get it. Those that don't get it and still ascend into leadership roles seem to do so by default; either they were good technicians or they made it to the top by being a leadership clone of their mentor, who was successful. In either case, they got there despite their trashy leadership style.

Over my career I have been subordinate to leaders in the military, manufacturing, education, health care, and volunteer organizations. I have led within those arenas as well; small teams, an elementary school staff of thirty, board chair of a community hospital, a fifteen person professional HR staff, and where it all began, a division of 180 sailors in the engineering department of an aircraft carrier.

Good leaders can be recognized immediately, since they get good work from their subordinates and their organizations show it. Less effective leaders get resistance and pushback from their folks (sometimes very subtly). The organization of a poor leader appears, on the surface, to be moving forward, but underneath it, work is slowed significantly. Associates do not take risks or question ideas. Time is wasted talking with others about the latest situation that occurred that they know about, which supports the suspicion of tyranny.

It is easy to tell which organization is which by watching subordinate's expressions when the leader's name is mentioned. If the leader is the problem, most associates are quietly polite and try to mask their feelings, while others are more open. If they are proud of their leader, they will tell you in a heartbeat.

The purpose of this book is to share some of the traits of leadership that I have observed and the lessons I have learned over a forty-year career. While my intended audience is primarily new managers like the one in the administrative department of the hospital, it will also be useful to experienced managers who often can use a word of encouragement when they find themselves struggling with problem associates. Those people are challenging the leadership for the very heart and soul of their organization.

The toughest minded among you may question some of my observations. I will point out, however, that if you are leading only from power, then you could be doing better. If you are interested in improving, read on. If you are looking for a leadership panacea, look elsewhere. Improving your leadership skills is not embracing a guru who has had a revelation from watching other organizations. It is taking advantage of experience and doing something about it. Improving as a leader starts with making a decision to change your leadership behavior because you don't like what is happening in your leadership life right now. Making that change happen is hard work.

Books have been written about the leadership qualities of Abraham Lincoln, Dwight D. Eisenhower, Franklin D. Roosevelt, Jesus Christ, and others. These works are about great men who applied sound leadership principles in shaping and molding large numbers of people from diverse backgrounds into successful entities that accomplished great things. Read those books too. There is a common thread among them:

Leadership is the artful application of interpersonal relationships built on some very sound principles.

A leader must make a conscious decision on how to lead, sometimes on an hour-by-hour basis.

I have grouped my list of leadership principles together as chapters, since they fit the mold of leadership that I have found to be the most effective, both as a follower and as the person in charge. I have found that if the core leadership principles are in place, outstanding performance—which is the logical extension of good leadership—will follow.

1

Honesty, Credibility and Respect

An inherent characteristic of American workers is that they want to respect and to be respected by the people who are in charge. It doesn't matter what type of organization they belong to; it can be manufacturing, health care, education, for profit, not for profit—it makes no difference. This desire for respect is evident in politics, in the workplace, in the home, and in the military. We tend to be snobs about how we are led, and why not? Part of our dynamic as a culture is rooted in the Declaration of Independence and our Constitution. We revere independence and independent thinking and we want to be treated according to those principles and values.

American workers continuously test the style and techniques of our leaders to be sure that the manner in which we are being asked to get tasks done hits the leadership target as we perceive it. Leadership activities are being questioned all the time, whether it is within a church, on a soccer field or in the workplace. Our legacy of rugged individualism and independence requires us to appropriately challenge our leaders constantly.

Honesty....

Honesty is at the top of my leadership model. Clearly, those being led insist on being told the truth consistently and without exception. Many leaders are not intentionally dishonest, but many do "spin" their actions and distort reality so that it takes on their meaning. Some politicians are masters of spin and some folks within the management community have learned the art of spin equally well. They may speak with fingers crossed at times, not because they are congenital liars but because they feel it is the lesser of two evils—the evil of spinning or their perceived evil of telling the bold truth and then living with unfavorable consequences. They often become guilty of selective truth telling.

There is a moral compass within each of us, and its little needle swings back and forth as we move through life. Sometimes that needle is steady, and sometimes it constantly moves in search of the magnetic north (being treated fairly and honestly), where we want it to stay. The desire to be on a moral course is a value for working America. Honesty is part of that moral aid to navigation that guides us through the seas of life—especially work life.

Organizations often do not tell the truth when they downsize. The guise under which they restructure is sometimes stated as a lack of sales or other business reasons (e.g. changing market focus). When the decision is made to make a reduction in force, however, they seize the opportunity to "take out" some poor performers, some independent thinkers, and those workers being paid high salaries who are filling lesser valued positions in the process. While that may be understandable, from a business standpoint, had the leadership been honest and doing its job along the way the poor performers would have been dealt with as the performance issues were noted; the independent thinkers would have been creatively tapped as a resource and their behavior channeled into productive endeavors; and the positions filled with those who are perceived as overpaid would not exist. That is, if the truth were told.

What is made public, however, is the claim that the reduction in force, or RIF, is related to a lack of sales, when in reality it also gives cover to solve some personnel problems that have not been dealt with effectively in the past. Too often the casualties are some very senior people who are blind-sided and will have difficulty finding similar work in the future. While there is a basic business truth in the need for the RIF, there are half-truths uttered to cover for some of the unexplained departures that should have been dealt with earlier. The unexplained departures are understandable if you are privy to the work histories or incidents involving the individuals who were let go, but making up for poor performance management during a RIF due to poor business conditions is a lie. Employees know that.

Has the leader told the truth? Perhaps, but they have not told the *whole* truth. And while airing dirty laundry is not appropriate, what is also not appropriate is telling associates good things about their performance during performance evaluations and coaching opportunities when something else should have been communicated. People get very defensive about their work, and it is not always easy to approach subordinates on the subject of improvement, but improving performance is what good leaders do. To sweep needed performance improvement under the rug is dishonest.

Credibility...

Closely related to honesty is credibility. This is another cardinal leadership characteristic to cultivate. Honesty is telling the truth. It is black and white. To your subordinates, you are either honest or you are not. Credibility has to do with perception and style, which for a leader is huge. When "your" people (those that you have been chosen to lead) believe that what you are doing and saying is the truth and is essential to them and the mission of the organization, credibility becomes a bond that you, as their leader, have established. Believing that the leader will carry out the organization's plans and that they will react responsibly and predictably (credibly) goes to the heart of leadership. Without credibility, the leader becomes perceived as a tyrant and work is done grudgingly, if at all.

Perception comes from the manner in which the message is communicated. Credible leaders are honest, but sometimes honest leaders are not credible. It is how they tell the story or how the truth plays out over time that gives meaning to credibility. In the context of leadership, a credible message is sent from the leader and received by the subordinate without any interpretation or question as to its truthfulness. Without credibility, the message is filtered by the listener for ulterior motives, hidden agendas, and assayed for the truth. A credible message is delivered and acted upon quickly and efficiently. To have credibility is to possess a direct link to the minds and hearts of the people, which if nothing else creates a culture of mutual understanding. It also creates a culture that works smoothly and effectively.

My definition of credibility also includes commitment. It is not enough to sound good; the leader has to prove them self repeatedly that they are always truthful and that they always have the best interests of the organization, and therefore its people, at heart. This means that the credible leader is committed to both the people and the organization and represents the best interests of both.

The art of gaining credibility (and it is an art) is not a "love at first sight" response. Although some humans communicate more effectively than others (practicing good communication leads to establishing credibility), there has to be give-and-take over time—a tension between message sender and message receiver which is always being tested. Reliable truth-telling proves to those being led that the leader, in fact, is credible—that they will act in a consistent and predictable manner. While "walking the talk" is the most common example of establishing credibility, the choice of words, as well as the manner in which they are spoken and the body language used while delivering the message, are also a part of gaining credibility. Once credibility is established, trust (the "T" word) develops over time. Having the trust of an organization is the mark of a great leader. Trust is powerful.

Watch the body language...

A young supervisor I knew was an honest and sincere person, but he had a nervous habit of speaking to people while he had a subtle smile on his face. As he talked, he would often tap a pencil if he held one, or he would tap his foot. These were gestures rooted clearly in nerves and anxiety. While his message was sincere, the body language was an indicator of discomfort, and to some it was interpreted as being untruthful. To the group he was addressing, the smile was not seen as a connecting gesture between the two; it was seen as a smirk, and the tapping was an indication to the people that he was not telling the whole truth. These nervous "ticks" gave him credibility problems.

These behaviors frequently disappeared when he got into the body of his message, especially if he was challenged and had to answer questions. At that point he would take on the demeanor of someone who believed in his message and become forceful instead of tentative. This supervisor struggled with developing rapport with his team until he got to know them and was more comfortable with them. Then the smirk-like smile faded and the tapping stopped. But put him in front of a new group and the anxiousness reappeared all over again and the process of establishing trust and credibility began anew. He had a problem he had to fix.

Another supervisor with whom I worked would deliver his message, whether it was for work assignments or outlining a new policy, in very stilted and formal language. When challenged as to why the new policy was needed, he used a tone of voice and language that sent a strong message that he did not want to discuss the matter. The effect was that the listeners would assume the worst. They just knew that there was some ulterior motive or hidden agenda that was being carried out. Why else would he not entertain questions on the subject? In reality, this too was a sign of uneasiness and discomfort with having to deliver potentially bad news to a group of associates. He had to become more open and receptive to interplay between himself and his work group. Until he changed that behavior, he had a credibility problem that bogged down his everyday supervisory chores.

Still another supervisor would stand in front of his associates, deliver his message using clear language, sincere tones and entertain questions to which he would give honest and straightforward answers and admit it when he did not know what the answer was if that was the case. His selection of words, tone of voice, and body language with his displayed interest in their concerns gave him credibility. He came across to his associates as sincere.

Another example is the leader who knew the group to whom he was speaking quite well. He would deliver a message on a new company policy that he was sure they would not want to hear. Instead of delivering a formal announcement, he began his message by saying something like, "Folks, we have a challenge to face today; if I had a choice of doing this or not, I would just as soon not, but the facts speak for themselves. We have to change what we have been doing before we can move on." His message was delivered in a serious tone using short, crisp sentences, and spoken with carefully chosen, sincere words. It was his style, and his people knew he could be trusted. He had a history of keeping his word. And while they didn't like what they heard, the messenger was not held responsible for the message.

Improve your communication style...

Clearly the first step is to carefully assess the manner in which you convey messages. The second, then, is to rehearse in front of an audience to develop a style that delivers both the spoken and unspoken (body language) message with clarity and sincerity: credibility. The next step is to replicate steps one and two over and over when needed to establish a long pattern of truth-telling and dependability.

An approach that is a favorite of teachers who have polished their craft of communicating work assignments to oftentimes unwilling children is also a useful model. Rather than a formal declaration given in the form of an announcement, an effective method is to engage the class in a brief conversation in very low tones about some unrelated topic. Then in the same tone of voice and with the same language, segue into the perceived unpleasant message. I have seen it happen many times.

Picture this: As her class assembles, Mrs. Jones is standing in the front of the room as she watches students come in and take their seats. There is the normal amount of hubbub as she engages a nearby student in a conversation about a sports event in low, conversational tones. As more students come in, she enlarges the circle of conversation by including the newly-arriving students by name, still maintaining the conversational style. At this point she has not gone into her "command" voice, the one she uses for giving directions.

After bantering with the students, Mrs. Jones begins to segue from the non-work related conversation to the learning tasks at hand. She makes the transition from casual language to the day's assignments while she remains in this "level" tone of voice—very conversational, but obviously louder so all can hear who are listening and attending to her. She is in control and she is showing she is in control by not reacting to the surroundings if they become noisy or emotional.

Perhaps several minutes have passed. If there is unacceptable banter, she pauses, slows her speech and looks in the direction of the unacceptable behavior. There is a silent tension between the teacher with credibility—one who is firm, fair, and trusted—and the students who are vying for the attention of the class. Her voice is not raised. She doesn't have to raise it. She has won this battle before many times, and she will win it again if she holds to her principles. Suddenly the entire class is attending to her.

Now that she has everyone's attention, she begins giving the messages necessary to get work started within the class. She has built rapport with the group and has set the example of voice tone and word choice to get the class going.

This style works 80 to 90 percent of the time with children and with adults too. It is effective if they are conditioned to reacting to instructions given by a teacher (leader) who demonstrates confidence and develops rapport with her group and establishes credibility.

Suzette Elgin, in her book *Success with the Gentle Art of Verbal Self Defense,* explains that there are five distinct modes that are used by humans in conflict. The type of language and behavior used in the example of Mrs. Jones, the teacher, is typical of what Elgin calls Leveling Mode. "Leveling" is where the speaker tells the truth as she understands it in low to normal voice patterns and tones, using low levels of body language and controlled behavior. A leader who conducts them self in a manner that utilizes leveling language exudes credibility. It can be taught; it can be learned.

Some might think my example of Mrs. Jones is unrealistic in today's fast-paced world of work, but it has been used repeatedly and occurs daily when there needs to be a transition from either lightheartedness or tenseness to reality. Credible leaders know how to use their voice tones and word selection to make their message the most important words that the followers will hear.

Credibility is more that staying on message; it is also staying on behavior. The leader who is predictable is also credible; they go together. Credibility must be earned over time so that those being led establish a feeling of shared confidence in the supervisor's ability to lead.

Telling the truth is at the heart of good leadership.

Truth is very fragile. If the chain of honesty is interrupted once—it is hard, if not impossible—to regain honesty as a personal quality of the leader. To be considered an honest person, one cannot knowingly be dishonest, ever, or not tell the truth, even once. To be caught in a lie is to lose credibility instantly, and it usually means it has been lost forever with that group.

A senior leader at one organization that I served gave me every reason to believe that he was honest. He never gave me any indication that what he said to me was not one hundred percent on track as far as honesty was concerned. I am sure he did not tell me everything he knew on a given subject, but what he did tell me I felt I could take to the bank.

However, in the heat of a discussion one day, he broke that trust—the linkage I had made between him and the truth—when he told me that if confronted over a given issue by a specific person, he was prepared to lie about it. Instantly his credibility was gone in my eyes. I continued to deal with him because I respected his position as my superior, but I never again trusted him to tell me the truth. The armored car of truth had just been hijacked on its way to the bank. That was too bad, for I am sure that for him, telling me he was prepared to lie was a brief moment of self disclosure for his own protection, but to me the trust was gone.

There are confessed liars everywhere, I have learned. I was mediating a dispute between two young women (essentially over a shared male friend) when after about forty-five minutes into the session the "victim" turned to me very candidly and very seriously said, "You know, I have been known to lie before. That is why she doesn't believe me now." That moment of self-disclosure was very revealing. The two who were in conflict came to terms with their work situation, but the "congenital liar" knew her word was meaningless. How then could someone in a leadership position even think they deserve any trust if they have a known habit of not telling the truth?

Treat people with dignity and respect...

Respect is sometimes a forgotten ingredient in the entrée of credibility. One of the core values of companies, certainly of professionally run human resource departments, is to treat people with dignity and respect. You hear it often. It flows. Those words go together, but they are quite different and take separate actions to cover both concepts. Treating someone with dignity means to not embarrass them; to not put them down. Showing dignity means to allow them to hold their head up high in all situations, and certainly in the face of unpleasantness. It means not taking some overt action or to go out of our way to make a spectacle of them. We tend to understand the concept of treating people with dignity. Respect, on the other hand, is tougher to apply consistently, but it is worth the effort.

Sometimes treating a person in a non-respectful way happens when we don't mean to. It is often a sin of omission. Respect in the context of the workplace does not mean to stand in awe of someone as we would the president. It does not mean to pay homage. Respect in the context of leadership means simply to give credit where credit is due.

If we act as if someone is not present when they physically are there, simply by not acknowledging them or making eye contact, we have been disrespectful. Caucasians do not often experience this "looking past" behavior that people of color report that they frequently experience. "Looking past" often happens in lines at a store or other similar gatherings. Not looking at someone is a sign of disrespect. That act tends to marginalize the other. It is an indicator that will be tested as the relationship develops. Check it out. If someone doesn't acknowledge you when they can't help but know you are there, it makes one feel insulted.

The same is true as we interact with departments within our organization in our daily work. When getting your work done requires that you venture into the work area of another person or department, to not acknowledge this intrusion is a sign of disrespect. To not recognize the experience of an associate when it comes to a particular topic or subject that they have been involved with before does not show respect for them. This kind of behavior marginalizes people and does not allow them to maintain their dignity (that other word). We say we forget, but in forgetting we have reduced ourselves in their eyes.

Something as simple as saying "hello" or "good morning" shows respect, since it acknowledges the presence of the other. Using language that is inclusive or shows sensitivity rather than being dismissive shows respect. Unfortunately, we often get tangled up in our interpretation of what is politically correct, and we do not use inclusive language. Don't let being politically *in*correct become a stumbling block in your relationship with your subordinates. Language is powerful.

Respect is playing by the rules. Respect is honoring the policies of other organizations, which in turn shows respect for its members. Respect is acknowledging the presence of a subordinate or a person of lower status from within the hierarchy of the work setting. Respect is saying "thank you" often. Respect is offering gentle reminders instead of giving orders. The list goes on.

In passive-aggressive cultures, which are common within health care, subtle messages continually flow back and forth between adversaries without a word being uttered. They purposefully do not say or do things to send messages. The feeling of the initiator must be that being verbally honest and open might spill over into patient care areas and be heard by someone who is not supposed to hear it. Perhaps being direct would seem unprofessional. Sometimes messages are then conveyed by not doing things or acknowledging someone in order for the person, so burdened, to get their point across. Unfortunately, some care providers have become masters of disrespect by simply doing their job with little or no acknowledgement of the patient. This probably has been efficient behavior in the past, but it robs the patient of dignity by not paying respect to them. Thankfully, that behavior has been identified as out-of-date. Organizations that flourish in the future will be those that treat all customers with respect…and dignity…because to do otherwise will force their customers to a competitor. There are choices.

Remember that you are leading fragile beings…

It is easy for supervisors to become so preoccupied with their busyness that they forget the simple things. Smiling, nodding, acknowledging, and paying attention are all a part of respecting the individual. Leaders who practice these behaviors win the confidence of their people. They set a tone for the group, and they are rewarded by faithful followers. Good teachers do this continually to build confidence and self-esteem in those fragile and developing personalities. I learned through working twenty-five years in industry (with a 12-year career as a middle school teacher sandwiched between years eight and 20) that adults are not that much different than kids when it comes to responding to good leadership. If you agree that to acknowledge others and listen to them is ok for teachers of small children but not for adult leaders, think again. Respect is respect is respect. We all need and expect it at any age.

Taking respect to a higher level includes remembering birthdays, anniversaries, how many children a parent has and what their names are. It may also include knowing, when appropriate, who is hurting from some home situation and why. The key here is to know with whom to talk about what as it applies to their daily lives. Some people need that kind of support, others do not want it, or at least indicate either verbally or non-verbally that they do not want to be involved in those conversations.

Change...a challenge to everyone...

In a manufacturing organization which I served, on the first business day of the New Year we returned to work after the holiday and were notified that we had been bought in an asset buyout (which is not as employee friendly as a stock purchase). The new owners were on-site and promptly fired the seven most senior officers of the company. That obviously left some very big holes in the organization. Those positions were filled by promoting some of us who were in the next tier down to those newly vacant leadership positions. The ensuing four months became a test for all of us as to whether or not this "shotgun wedding" would work.

There were, of course, new policies and new strategies. We went through downsizing due to product line adjustments. I understood that.

As Human Resources Director, I was given new guidelines in the area of salary increases. We were to toe the line at 3%. This had always meant that to maintain a three percent average increase, some got zero and some got six. I found out later that was not what the new CEO meant at all.

He also asked that he initial every increase that was submitted through our merit increase system. This was a level of scrutiny that I was not used to, but I understood the need to build confidence and credibility on both sides. If he wanted to initial every increase, so be it. The first batch of approximately seven change-of-status forms went to the president's office for his signature to adhere to this new procedure. The next day he came into my office carrying the COS forms in his hand and slammed them down on my desk. "I thought I said no more than three percent for any of these people," he said as he glared at me. "Some of them are four and five percent."

"Sorry, boss," I said. "My understanding was they should average three percent over the year. There are some very valuable people in that group that need to be taken care of," I continued.

"Tom, you don't understand," he said in a firm voice. "The less for them, the more for us."

What would have been your reaction to that statement? How would you have responded to your relatively new leader when his strategy was very simply to play employees against each other for his/our personal gain?

My response was simply, "I understand the concept, but that is not my style. Please, leave me out of any bonuses based on that logic."

He was stunned. He took the COS forms back to his office and looked at them a second time. They came back the next day the way I sent them to him in the first place. I had won my argument, but that confrontation started my search to leave that organization—not because I thought the company was bad or wrong, but because my leader made a very strong statement about his honesty and credibility. I could not defend him to myself or to others after that incident. It was impossible for me to get his words out of my mind. Nothing he said to me in the future could undo the philosophical knot with which he had tied our relationship.

Honesty is the one value that is never, ever compromised.

2

Empathy, Caring and Sincerity

Work is hard. We talk about work being fun, and if you are able to perform the tasks that generate value to your organization in an enjoyable manner and get paid for it, that is great. Likewise, being a leader is not pleasant and fun all the time either. Leader-work means keeping ones guard up, which can cause tension and stress...never being able to let down. In addition, a leader must be approachable day in and day out, even if they don't feel like it. Being a leader is not always easy; that is why we call it work. To the leader, work means putting forth a pleasant front while interrelating with employees in a positive, upbeat manner when you would rather not. It is part of the job.

When I was starting my business career at Campbell Soup, the comptroller at the plant where I was working described one of his managers as having great equanimity. They didn't get rattled and always presented themselves as calm and in control. I had never thought of a personal trait quite in those terms before, but equanimity hits the leadership mark quite well. Leadership also has to do with personal interaction and relationship building. Leadership encompasses treating each individual according to their personality and their needs, day in and day out.

The three words that describe this chapter are empathy, caring, and sincerity. They are interrelated and will be addressed as one concept here. The bonding agent that ties these three together is persistence. Showing empathy to a person once may not mean you have gained their seal of approval forever. While you can probably display a caring attitude most of the time, you do not get a prize for being a caring leader for "most of the time." If you come across as insincere, just once, you may have damaged your credibility and it might take months to rebuild it. Being known as a caring leader that appropriately shows empathy and sincerity requires a personal pattern of behavior that some leaders just have not developed. Some of us are not hard wired to consistently have our guard up so we have to work at it constantly—every day. That is where persistence comes in.

Talking to your people about personal things...

Supervisors I have known handle this phase of relationships with their people differently, depending on their style. One supervisor I knew dispensed with these three behaviors altogether. He did not know when to appropriately show empathy, and since it can be emotionally draining, he chose not to "do empathy." He showed little or no emotion to anyone at any time, thus he never came across as caring. It was just the way he was. It does not make his style a preferred model, however. Just the opposite is true. When times got tough, when there were great issues facing his team, his no-nonsense, take-no-prisoner style kept him and his team from performing at the top of their game. There was too much tension and resentment clouding the atmosphere for that team to remain effective through the tough times. If someone in the group was experiencing a personal tragedy, time was wasted by those who knew about it by talking to anyone who would listen as to how insensitive their supervisor was. The leader's behavior became the issue instead of the employee's problem. The group would collectively pout for days about the boss's insensitivity, and as a result their performance suffered.

This same supervisor was being coached by his superior to improve his interpersonal skills. One can only imagine how the coaching session went, but it must have sounded something like this: "Phil, you have got to loosen up. Your people are complaining that you do not care about them as individuals. Take some time to get to know them. Ask them about their families." To which Phil must have replied, "Yes, sir. Whatever you say, boss. I hear you."

The next day, Phil was giving directions in his no-nonsense manner when he remembered his boss's order to loosen up. He jumped to his senses and tried to use a little of his new-found caring attitude. His comments to his subordinate came out like this: "Jean, I want you to go over to the next station and help the people over there. You have not finished this job yet, but they need you now. What you are working on can wait. That order is not due for two more days. So, how's your sister?"

As insincere as this example sounds, it actually happened and is probably happening repeatedly throughout the day in workplaces everywhere. A casual question tacked on to a long instruction that is neutral, at best, will not be perceived as sincere. The only way this "quick question" interaction works is if the supervisor has a long history of discussing the sister and her health and a new twist recently in her condition took place. This was his first try, and it came out as an afterthought. In Phil's case, he would be smart to lead with the discussion of the sister and then finish with the instruction. If the leader is going to take a stab at caring by inquiring into the health of one's family member, he must come across as genuine, or else the question should be left unasked.

If you are one of those "get the job done at all cost" leaders and you do not segue well from giving instructions to asking personal questions, you need to develop a new technique. What you are doing now is killing the performance of your team.

Know when enough is enough...

Just as Phil came across as insincere, there are leaders who pry too much. Developing a sense of what is appropriate to ask and when is a conversational art leaders must develop. People who do not have this behavior down pat should practice it before they try it out in the real work world. They should develop some verbal "safe havens" and practice them before they become too glib with their folks. To be "glib" means that it leaves the feeling with the associate that you are asking just because you think you should.

The phrase "I feel your pain" has become so hackneyed and hollow that I personally stay away from those words at all costs. Just like saying "Have a nice day" is meant to be a friendly parting comment, too often it sounds hollow because it is over-used. However, a word of encouragement speaks to people. Carve out your own phrases that mean the same thing and use them. Find words of encouragement that fit your style.

The knowledgeable leader makes time to talk to their people every day; and they does so in private. "Private" means not in front of others; it does not have to be behind closed doors if the information does not warrant that level of privacy. "Face time" is what some people crave with their boss. When starved of that intimacy, "the folks" begin to resent personal questions. "If you didn't care about my problems last week, why are you interested this week?" seems to be their feeling. Keeping in touch is essential, much as a parent will stay up-to-date with their child's activities.

There are times when probing personal questions may be appropriate. If the employee's normal work performance changes, checking out the reason is in line. Absenteeism, tardiness, or low productivity might be caused by a sudden illness of a parent or child or some other factor emanating from home. The key is their performance. They can tell you the details or not, but at least you have appropriately opened the dialog. Regardless of the reason, they should be made aware that their work is slipping.

Make your rounds. Talk to them. Mosey with them. Learn about them. To the extent that they are willing to share personal information with you, get to know your people. Never press for more than they are willing to share, but at the same time, if a situation is hurting their performance, press the discussion. The reason for their substandard performance is a legitimate question that should be asked. If it is too personal (such as marriage problems) and you can do nothing about it, fair enough. Don't go down that road. At least you have opened the dialog and given them a chance to explain themselves and you have the chance to offer Employee Assistance Program services if that benefit is available.

Building strong work relationships with those we lead is an essential part of being an effective leader. Understanding what each person needs is the distinction between a run-of-the-mill supervisor and a respected leader. The term "situational leadership" comes to mind here, which simply means knowing each person well enough to be able to motivate them to achieve their potential. With that knowledge in mind, the appropriate level of supervision can be rendered for the set of conditions that are present.

Know what you are talking about...

Knowing how to be empathetic can only come with experience. If a member of your team is struggling with a teenager and your children are not yet in that age group, it is hard to show the appropriate under-standing and level of concern. A similar situation exists when dealing with death, especially the death of parents, mates or children. Unless you have lost a close relative, it is difficult to show the appropriate level of empathy that this event deserves. For that reason, I would counsel that you don't try to be all-wise and understanding. Instead, acknowl-edge the loss both verbally and in writing and if the relationship war-rants, praise their strength during this difficult time. The last thing you should do is to share an experience that is a peg or two lower on the life scale of significant events that they are experiencing. That type of expression degrades the situation they are experiencing, and with that your stature slips in their eyes. Sometimes saying little or nothing is best, depending on how they process grief. Regardless of the circum-stances, I have learned to always acknowledge the loss in writing.

The key is to know your associate well enough so you understand how they will handle the loss. If you don't have any clues on how the loss affects them, say very little about it, but say something. Be careful; you may be making a wrong assumption.

If you know the person well and if you do have a truly comparable experience (i.e. you have lost your parents and one of theirs has just died), indicate to them that you realize how great a loss it is. I have found the words, "It is never easy losing a parent, under any conditions" to be an opener for conversation. Those words apply to sudden death, long drawn out death when that is the only relief from suffering, and to traumatic death. Follow up the previous comment to correlate to what type of situation your team member faces—something like "And you are setting the standard in dealing with your loss." Never tell someone about how your parent died while they are grieving. This is their moment, their loss…don't marginalize it. There will be time for your stories later, when they begin to process the loss and can put it into perspective and talk about death philosophically.

The challenge that leaders face in dealing with associates who are suffering is to know when to show empathy, when to be caring and sincere, and when to push the associate to heal, get better, and move on. There is both healing and strength in maintaining a routine and trying to function normally. It is not always easy to tell when to maintain a high level of understanding or to begin to get the associate back to a work routine. Seek advice from an experienced leader or mentor. My experience is to give a troubled associate plenty of leeway. Tell them that you are going to work with them during this hard time and then begin to set standards for when "normal" should return. In the case of divorce, this could be a three or four month process. Probably the most difficult situation to gauge is the serious illness or injury of a child. If it is severe enough (e.g. auto accident), it may take months for this process to stabilize. While the Human Resource policy that your organization has for these situations may give you guidance, their individual circumstance will be a topic of discussion among team members for a long time. Don't hide from it. Invite discussion. Listen, learn, and be as open as you feel you can be with them.

The personal experiences that I shared in this chapter told of leaders who are caring, who wish to show the appropriate empathy, and who want to do so in a sincere manner. My suggestions will not work if there is not a wellspring of trust already established between the leader and the subordinate, and that wellspring does not develop quickly; it has to be nurtured. Honesty and the ability to listen effectively are the two best attributes in dealing with employees who are going through difficult times. But dare to take the step. Dare to initiate the conversation. Dare to lead.

3

Consistency, Fairness and Predictability

The one trait that subordinates look for and appreciate—and I might add demand from their leaders—is consistency. Even the toughest policies can be accepted if they are applied uniformly. Here is the rub: The one thing that you as a leader prize most is flexibility, which runs counter to consistency at times. Consistency on the one hand, flexibility on the other; that creates tension. Just understand that associates are watching you closely to see how you will make the call. When can and should you make exceptions to policy? The quick answer is "never." Being consistent and applying policies uniformly to your subordinates is a cardinal rule that should never be broken...almost.

Hear me out on this. The rule is "be consistent," but there are times when you must be flexible. These times include truly unique situations—those with a high likelihood of not being repeated—or if they do come up again, the conditions and therefore the precedence you have set in the first situation most likely will not be replicated.

There are times when policies, as well thought out and written though they may be, do not speak directly to a specific situation. The exception may be when you have to live within a union contract, then your interest about being flexible or making allowances for good performers will most likely not be possible. Even with a tightly-worded contract, there are times when exceptions should be considered to serve the intent of the contract, if not its letter. In this case, get help from your HR department. A good leader will at least pursue the possibility of trying to help a good performer.

During my tenure as labor relations manager of a manufacturing facility of about 500 union employees, I learned that each one of those 500 had a "consistency" measuring device clipped on their belt. They were not afraid to get it out in a heart beat to see if the standard used in their situation or one they knew about was the same standard that had been most recently applied to someone else they knew. If there was a discrepancy, the rank and file would assault the shop committee with questions, who in turn would be in my office demanding an explanation about the application of the work rule in question. If there was not a reasonable answer, it would be reduced to writing in the form of a grievance. If unresolved, it would proceed through the steps that included arbitration. Consistency is that important. If the shop committee could somehow be made to see the logic of the action and the application of the rules were consistently applied, or would in the future be similarly applied, we could often get resolution to a sticky problem.

Stick to your guns...

There are times when a rule must never be broken. The most common example is tardiness. If you have a policy that gives little latitude for being late to work, a leader must first adhere to it himself, and second, apply it uniformly in all cases. Wavering back and forth about absenteeism and tardiness is lethal to the morale of a tight knit organization.

One example involved a human resource generalist, a very competent person who had a bad habit of getting to work late. Not significantly late, mind you, but just past starting time. He might only be ten minutes late, but he was consistent. He lived the furthest from work of any of the staff and at first it appeared as though he was just having trouble gauging his travel time and allowing for traffic or weather conditions, but the tardy behavior kept on. In a five-day period he was tardy three days. When he arrived at work, he made no attempt to apologize or to even acknowledge that he was finally at work or say "hello." He would just come in and get to work.

This behavior continued for several months following his departmental orientation when his supervisor took the opportunity to remind him (not yet knowing of his tardiness problem) that the HR staff lived in a fish bowl. Other departments were watching the HR department's behavior on a number of areas such as dress code (denim jeans, anyone?) and tardiness. He acknowledged that he understood what this meant and vowed that he would be a model employee. In fact, he was very good about staying late to finish projects or continuing to make phone calls to check references. But enough was enough. He needed to understand that coming to work late was unacceptable. What ensued became a six month battle of wills. He would at the same time acknowledge that good employees should follow the rules, but he also maintained that he was not a morning person and had a long way to drive and just couldn't seem to do any better. Some rules just did not apply to him.

During this time, two hourly HR assistants began to show up four to seven minutes late for work. They were counseled about their tardiness. In both cases, they mentioned—nicely mind you—that the salaried person did it all the time. They were assured that he was being appropriately dealt with too. Of course they knew he was staying late, but the yardstick being used was this: be on task at 8:00 a.m. It was a tough six months. It ended when Mark gave notice that he was resigning for a job closer to home. A good leader will confront unacceptable behavior, no matter whose it is.

Being consistent is tough. It is making sure that all the rules apply uniformly. It is also confronting behavior that is not acceptable within the organization. Even though others in the organization may tolerate tardiness, for example, it should be confronted, because it is not fair to those who make the effort to be at work on time. Consistency is worth pursuing to the end.

Men are so predictable…women leaders should be too!

Predictability is both a virtue and a vice. Ask any woman how men will react in a given circumstance and you will hear their favorite repose, "Men are so predictable." When it comes to the battle of the genders, it is often well to be unpredictable, but in the work place—be you male or female—your people want, and a good leader should exude, predictability.

One of the tenants of teamwork is knowing what another person will do in a given situation. You can call it anticipation, if you like. Often it is referred to as being able to complete the other's sentences. It all falls under the same big, soft, comfortable quilt: predictability. It is a virtue, because it gives a semblance of order to the chaos of the day. It is a security blanket during those harried moments that occur in any organization when things seem to unravel. Knowing what the leader will do in a clutch situation is comforting, soothing, and reassuring.

I attended a week long seminar on Labor Relations at the University of Michigan. My assistant, Lisa, was left to "fend off the wolves" in my absence. If there were any employee relations problems, she was to log in the complaint and do the best she could at resolving the easy ones and refer the rest to the VP. Of course the goal was to not have to take anything to the VP, but had it been a catastrophe, she would gladly throw it "upstairs."

When I returned from the week away, my first task was to consult with Lisa as to how the week without me had been (these were the days prior to cell phones and voice mail). She smiled and simply said, "I handled them all. I have heard you tell people with similar problems the same answers many times, so I just told them what I thought you would have said." Lisa was right on. Had I been all over the board about decisions, she would not have known how to respond to a given situation. Since I was predictable, she simply applied the known logic to the situations that came to her. She had done well.

On the shop floor or in the office, anticipating what the leader will do, say, or how they will react will keep the grapevine active if you are absent. An active grapevine is a bane to productivity. However, if you are predictable and forthright, productivity will not be affected at all, and if you have a union, predictability will keep the number of grievances down. People know what to expect and how to react. Those being led value your approval and will work hard to get it. Being predictable may not be romantic enough for your significant other, but that trait will hold you in good stead as a leader of human beings in the workplace.

4

Accountability, Performance and Work

"Where do you tell your family you are going when you put on your hat and coat and head out to Hart & Cooley? You tell them you are going to work. So, let's get to work!" I heard those words uttered by a first line supervisor in "real time" to an associate of his who was finding excuses to keep from having to perform his assigned tasks. This wasn't a novel quip, but it was quick and to the point. We all have tasks to perform on the job or else there would be no job. We call it "work," and while that sounds like drudgery, performing those tasks is why we have value and why we get paid.

A time-killing activity that some team members in the work setting actually expend brain power performing is playing "psych games" with their boss (their leader) to keep from having to perform their assigned tasks. This is a non-value added activity that literally sucks the strength out of an organization. What's more, supervisors let them get away with it. It all boils down to leadership.

Making assignments, setting expectations, and following up by measuring performance is what leaders get paid to do. That is our work in any organization. Sometimes included in this list of tasks is holding people accountable. However, accountability sometimes sets a tone of retribution. Sure, if the numbers do not add up properly (expectations are not met) over a long enough period of time (performance), something—or someone—has to change. But to give assignments and in the same phrase indicate that someone will be held accountable sounds like the Sword of Damocles is being held over their head, and that kind of leadership is counter productive. It causes stress and worry and is not conducive to a smooth, flowing team environment. To me, accountability is understood and goes along with giving expectations; it is better kept out of the conversation, at least in the early stages.

Ultimately, we are all accountable for our actions (work performance), but when a leader is trying to bring a team together—especially a new team—using the word "accountable" with the team is not a good way to start.

The disciplinary process...

Most organizations use a four-step process in removing someone from the job (firing them). First is verbal notification, which is often documented in writing just so there is a record of it. This serves as an initial indication that there is a problem. If discussions have taken place in the past, it is now time to make it clear that there is a genuine concern and that the supervisor is sincere. Going into the discipline process says that this is serious stuff.

If a verbal warning doesn't get the desired results (behavior change or performance improvement), a written notification or warning is given. At this point, the associate should be informed in very clear language that if improvement isn't made there is a very real possibility that they could lose their job (be fired).

The third step is sometimes a suspension from work. Suspensions have the same effect as a fine, since the associate loses pay (one day, three days, five days or two weeks). Sometimes organizations use a final written notice (not to be confused with a last chance letter), which in lieu of suspension has some extra teeth in it by stating in precise language what is expected both from a performance standpoint (which should be included in the first two steps as well) and with a very clear, precise penalty, including how long this document covers—one month, two months or six months—before the associate will be terminated (fired).

Obviously, the fourth step is termination—quick, swift, and final. Just leave. In his song *Fifty ways to leave your lover*, Paul Simon catalogs the manner in which separations can be carried out with the lyrics: "Slip out the back, Jack; Make a little plan, Stan; Don't need to be coy, Roy; Just listen to me. Get off the bus, Gus; Don't need to discuss much; Drop off the key, Lee; just set yourself free." The same phrases can apply to terminations. The time for negotiations is over.

I described the four-step process. Since the word "accountability" is very legalistic, it should be reserved for use in the disciplinary (four-step) context. Using the word accountability too soon and too often actually robs the leader of the flexibility they need to improve performance without the use of threats (and I feel strongly the use of the word accountability is a threat). Threatening someone's job is a last resort. I am all in favor of using clear language when setting expectations, however.

Here are some examples of giving good work assignments:

1. *Jim, I would like you to do an analysis of this proposal by making a spread sheet and make a comparison of the costs. You were able to make the last analysis in about two hours. Do you think that is reasonable for this one as well? I will check back with you in about half an hour to see how you are doing, but if you have any questions, please call me at once. This information is key to our presentation to senior management, which is coming up in two days.*

2. *Helen, please go over to press 956 and begin work on the order that has been set up. You have run this job before, but I want you to be sure to observe the safety requirements of this press while you are working. The standard on this job is 250 pieces per hour. Let me know when you are ready to start so I can check the safety switches and see how the first few pieces run. If you have any questions, please call me.*

Now compare good instructions with one that uses the word "accountable" in the process of giving instructions:

> *Dell, the balance sheet of our subsidiary poses several questions to me. Please look it over, make a list of questions you think need to be more clearly defined and let me know when you are ready to discuss this. If we agree on what information is missing, then you can call them and fill in the blanks. I am holding you accountable to get this thing in order before the management meeting Friday.*

Just listening to this makes me defensive. How about you? It sounds like Dell is given a very responsible job to get done, and if he doesn't measure up he will be demoted, fired, reprimanded, or who knows what else. Or if he doesn't get it done right, he is to blame. Is this what you want to convey? Threats stifle creativity. Is "holding them accountable" the way to get someone thinking on their own and willing to take risks or imagine a better way of doing things? I don't think so.

Do we use the word "accountable" too much?

Accountability should be an understood term in an organization, not one that needs to be used over and over. However, there are organizations where there has been little or no accountability displayed over time, and the performance of the organization shows. In this case, we go back to Chapter 3 on consistency and fairness. This organization did not get where it is in a week. It got there over time, and the leadership let (or led) it deteriorate, so the associates need to know the new rules and the new expectations that are being made. They should be given fair warning that if their performance does not measure up to the leader's new standard, there will be some discussion about accountability on a very private, one-on-one basis.

From a Human Resources point of view, performance improvement is why an HR department exists. Whether it is pay, benefits, training, staffing, performance reviews, whatever the function, HR's function is to improve productivity, however your organization measures it. There are leadership aids available and a good HR department will furnish them. Hopefully, you have that resource available to you.

What is a PIP?

Let us compare the use of the four-step disciplinary process that we described above with a performance improvement program, or PIP. I like to make the distinction between the two. While ultimately both the four-step disciplinary process and a performance improvement plan (PIP) end at the same place, someone can get fired, but up until they play themselves out the two processes (discipline for violation of a work rule and trying to improve performance through PIP) are different.

Make no mistake, associates will refer to them both as being "written up," but there is some traction to be gained in improving performance by separating the two. If associates feel that the supervisor can't be impartial, it is easier to become a victim under the disciplinary approach. ("She has it in for me.") If this is truly a performance problem which can be objectively identified and measured, under a PIP both the leader and the associate can focus on improvement. In reality, the reason a person's performance is poor may have to do more with not knowing what is expected or how to perform (lack of training) than it is about either not having the skill or willfully not performing the task. When improvement takes place, the associate can move forward without disciplinary notices littering their personal file. The downside results of both could be the same result: loss of their job. But there is a difference between a PIP and putting someone in the industrial due process system.

Under a PIP, the associate is given a chance to maintain their dignity and put the past behind them without disciplining them…if they improve. Also under a PIP, it may not require four steps to get to the termination if progress is not made. It could be cut to three or even two, or if performance is blatantly poor enough, one step.

Let's consider an example:

Sandra, an assistant in a Human Resources department, was assigned to support the employment staff by posting jobs, checking references, and maintaining applicant files. She is very social and entertained friends at her desk frequently. She also chaired a community committee and was on the phone more than most thought was appropriate. She is kindhearted, and when she worked she was like a person driven. But her customers (the staffing group), were not happy with her productivity. They complained to their boss. They wanted a change in her performance.

To solve this problem, Phyl (the manager) called the group together to discuss the flow of work among the four in the staffing group. Sandra's responsibilities were clarified with agreed upon timelines defined so that she was aware of what was expected. During the team meeting, Sandra became defensive when mention was made that her processes were not considered efficient by other staff members. One of them had covered for Sandra when she took a long weekend and reported that she got her work done in half the time that Sandra reported.

While that was a tense discussion, the meeting was closed with the view that Sandra would keep her paperwork current with a 24-hour turnaround.

Phyl decided to have a private meeting with Sandra to discuss the team meeting and to be sure that Sandra had a plan to improve.

At the start of the meeting, Phyl thanked Sandra for being positive throughout the discussions and encouraged her to voice her opinions whenever she felt she was being asked to do something that was not in the scope of her job. Phyl told Sandra that while she was concerned that everyone in the department managed their time appropriately, she needed to focus on improving the processes that the team had discussed.

Phyl then asked Sandra to tell her exactly what her approach was going to be to improve, including the time it would take to make the changes. While Sandra was engaged in the conversation and displayed an attitude of cooperation, there was a defensive tone in her voice and she talked about previous jobs she had held where she was considered a star performer. She also indicated that the other three people in the team did not always treat her with respect.

Phyllis listened to her, but then laid out the parameters of the agreement that the team had reached and that she and Sandra had discussed. Sandra became emotional and after one outburst of tears calmed down and said she knew what was going on, but that she would play the game. When asked what she meant, she simply stated that she felt the others wanted her fired and would do anything to see that it happened.

Phyllis took the opportunity to discuss the work of the department, the work of the staffing team and Sandra's role within the department. She told Sandra that the best outcome for everyone was a smooth running department with the current people doing the work. Sandra apologized for her outburst and said she would try to meet the expectations of her customers. The meeting ended with Phyllis telling Sandra that she would reduce to writing the performance items that had been discussed and the timelines that had been agreed to.

Dare to hold people accountable...

The next day, Phyl called Sandra into her office and presented her with a Performance Improvement Program that captured those items they had discussed the day before. Phyl had signed it and presented it to Sandra for her signature. As she took the letter from Phyl, Sandra once again talked about the petty animosities that surrounded the issues that she felt were at the heart of the team's concerns. Phyl reminded Sandra once again that this discussion was about her performance and how it influenced the work relationships within the team. She reminded her other concerns should be dealt with individually with the people involved. Sandra signed the PIP.

The PIP called for specific goals and timetables for performance improvement. It called for Phyl to monitor the process going forward and for Sandra to talk to her customers at least weekly to determine if their needs were being met. If the terms of the PIP were not met, Phyl would call a meeting with the team to discuss the issues. If there seemed to be improvement, Phyl would tell Sandra, and in either case, they would meet in thirty days to discuss the future. No mention was made that Sandra's job was at risk. Would this exercise get the job done?

Phyllis had a tough role. She had to step forward and hold Sandra accountable (notice the use here is implied and not spoken) for the agreement she signed. If Sandra does not perform, Phyl must take it to the next step, which is a second meeting. At that time she must remind Sandra that if her performance does not improve significantly in the immediate future she could lose her job. Sandra's success or failure depended on the satisfaction of her internal customers whom she thinks do not like her. Phyllis must keep performance separate from feelings and emotions. She owes it to Sandra, to the organization from a legal perspective, and to herself. If she has to terminate Sandra, she must have a clear conscience that she did her very best to help her improve. Sandra is going to require coaching to make her successful. It is Phyl's job to step up and be that coach whenever a question comes up about Sandra's work.

...but use the term "take ownership" instead.

When leaders put on their coaching hat, they assume much closer contact with the associate. They must become involved in the detail of their work and they have to be ready to pat them on the back for good performance and point out their shortcomings when performance slips. If Phyl truly wants to be a leader, she has a good opportunity to prove it by either making Sandra successful or terminating her in an ethical, legal and dignified way for the sake of the team. She must *Dare to Lead.* To do anything else would be to abdicate her role and duties as a leader.

To hold associates accountable is the role of the leader. To frequently remind them that they are accountable is tantamount to giving up your role as a creative leader and giving way to threatening language. At some point, fear takes over as the sole motivator and if the role of the leader is to get the best performance from her people and turn a C+ organization into an A organization, they will be successful only if fear and intimidation is removed. Fear, by its nature, is a limit on the growth of individuals. It slows processes and stifles creativity. Fear grows like a cancer throughout an organization if there are not clear expectations established that low performers will be dealt with humanely—with dignity and respect. If poor performance is dealt with randomly by the use of fear, it can paralyze the organization. Use terms like "take ownership" or "develop a sense of urgency" to convey the accountability message to the organization.

One leader I knew was fixated on the word accountability. He felt that the organization he inherited just went along doing what it always did and people were not motivated to improve. He targeted two of his managers so he could send a message and change the organization. When they were abruptly terminated, fear gripped the rest of the management group. While some had opinions as to the performance level of the pair, there had been no visible attempt to counsel them to get them to change. In fact, the grapevine had it that at least in one case, her subordinates actually met with the administrator and asked for her removal. It was a classic coup d'etat. In fact one of the subordinates was elevated to the manager position.

When word got back to the leader that there was great angst among the management team, at the next general leadership meeting he acknowledged that there would be change. In front of the group of sixty-plus managers he said, "It does not mean one strike and you were out, but you didn't get five strikes either." Many in the leadership team became paralyzed because of these comments. Due to the termination of the two and the manner surrounding one of them, the buzz that followed among the managers was "Who is the umpire, and who is keeping score (other departments or the senior leaders)?" What had started out as an attempt to motivate the management team turned into an employee relations disaster. Unfortunately, at a subsequent management meeting a projector failed and the administrator turned to his assistant and said, "Strike two." A hush fell over the room. His attempt at lightheartedness backfired.

Great performance comes from motivated people working in an environment of trust and openness. Great performance cannot be coerced. It takes leadership in the form of coaching, mentoring, supervising, and above all treating people fairly to turn average performers into a highly efficient team. I recalled the sound advice of my old skipper, Captain Miller: "A good ship is a happy ship." This was not a happy ship.

Where do you tell you family you are going when you put on your hat and coat each morning as you head out the door? You tell them you are going to work, and that is what your employer should expect from you: the traditional fair day's work for a fair day's pay. Communicating expectations and giving instructions is what leaders do, but a good leader does it in a way that maintains the dignity of the individual and shows respect for members of the team as persons and honors what they bring to the workplace. If you have organizational power, being a bully is easy, but in the long run bullying does not get the best results from people.

5

Servant Leadership

The term "Servant Leadership" came to my attention during the early 1990's. The concept was not new; in fact, it is Biblical in its origins. Among other places, Servant Leadership was popularized by the 1991 book authored by former Nixon assistant and now prison evangelist, Chuck Colson, in his book *Why America Doesn't Work*. It was written during a period of tough economic times when it appeared that we, as a country, were being economically gobbled up by Japan. While this did not prove to be the case, our then stagnant economy was producing ugly thoughts by many amateur economists (some felt that Japan had finally won World War II because they owned significant interests in U. S. banks). Because of this feeling, it became chic for employers to take out full page ads honoring their workforce and listing all members by name. The cut line was something to the effect that these Americans do work.

Colson's book was at the top of the reading list of senior management at the manufacturing business where I worked. During that time, the leadership team worked on a statement of core values. One of the ten values we chose to uplift was leadership, and within it was a reference to the term Servant Leadership. It stated: "We believe in using a participative approach, and that *leaders must be prepared to serve*, enabling others to meet their goals and encouraging them to achieve their potential in our pursuit of excellence."

As a result of that statement, I have fashioned my leadership style around those words and encourage others to do the same. I am amazed at how few manager/leaders recognize the term or have even thought about it. Some do not even understand what the term means. Because of Colson's book and our work on our leadership value, it became part of my personal definition of leadership.

Biblically, there are several references that I am aware of that discuss being great (a leader): Mark 10:43 "...To be great, first you must serve." Another is from Luke 22:26 "...the one who is greatest among you must become like the youngest, and the leader like the one who serves." Another is from John 13:5, "Then he poured the water into a basin and began to wash the disciples' feet and wipe them with a towel." In this example, the leader acts as the servant and "walks the talk."

Discovering Servant Leadership on a Navy ship...

How does this all fit together in the context of leadership in our American society? My first realization of what Servant Leadership meant was a very practical lesson, but I didn't recognize it as Servant Leadership until years later.

I was a newly commissioned ensign in the Navy assigned as Boiler Division Junior Officer onboard my first ship, an aircraft carrier. My duties were to learn the engineering plant of this huge ship, stand watches, and perform administrative duties.

B-Division, as we called it, was made up of about two hundred men (women did not serve in combatants in 1964), whose job it was to maintain and operate 12 oil-fired boilers that made steam to drive the four engines. Boiler tending is dirty, hot, and tiring work. One of the most disliked chores was taking a boiler (there were 12 and we used 8 or 10 at any given time) out of service and cleaning its insides.

A boiler is a big furnace with tubes full of water and steam running through it in a distinct pattern. Some tube configurations were in the shape of the letter D; ours looked like a big M. If sailors cleaned the tubes within the furnace that the flaming black oil touched, it was called cleaning "fire sides." If they cleaned inside the tubes and inside the big drum that the tubes were attached to, this was referred to as cleaning "water sides." Cleaning either water sides or fire sides was hot, dirty work.

When the sailors cleaned water sides, they first drained the big drum of all its water. Then they would unbolt a plate on the end of the water drum that covered an access hole that was barely large enough for a person to slide through. When the metal was cooled down enough to touch, they crawled inside the empty water drum and scraped the insides with a paint scraper and wire brush. This got rid of any accumulated residue (minerals and salts) from the water as it boiled to make steam. It was like cleaning the inside of a coffee pot or teakettle that had scale on it from the minerals in the water. The inside of the drum, when empty, was big enough for three average-sized people. It was tight.

The sailors expected that I (as their division junior officer or JO) would climb inside that water drum sometime during the cleaning process, since I was learning about the steam plant. I could delegate the chore and send someone else to inspect it to see how bad the scale was (there should not be much) and to see if the scale had been properly removed by all the scraping and chipping inside the boiler. Of course senior petty officers were the experienced hands who actually made the call, but as JO of the division, I was expected to learn these things first hand. It also gave me the opportunity to experience some of the hardships the sailors had to endure. In my mind, there was only one solution to the dilemma of whether or not I would delegate the inspection or do it myself. If I could climb around inside smelly silos and clean stables with a pitchfork on the farm at home, I could climb inside this boiler. I was going in. It was tricky because of my gangly size, but I made it.

Once inside, I asked the petty officer who was in charge of this work space to hand me the paper bag that I had brought along with me. From the bag I pulled about a half dozen sandwiches that had been prepared on the mess decks just minutes before. I knew I was destined for this experience, and on my way to the fire room I stopped in the crew's chow line (it was open all night while we were at sea conducting flight operations) and asked the cook to put together some sandwiches for my men. I climbed inside that boiler to pay a visit and learn, but first we would eat.

Those sailors never forgot that I brought them a treat that night. For the next two years that I served in Roosevelt, they would ask, "Did you bring sandwiches, Mr. Lutz?" Quite often I did stop by the chow line and bring a treat (usually sweet rolls hot out of the oven) to those doing the dirty work. In exchange, it became the custom of the men within the fire room that I visited to have a cup of coffee waiting for me when my feet hit the deck plates as I made my entrance. Their goal was to please me in exchange for my "servant leadership." There were other examples where I removed road blocks or made their lives more tolerable, but this one comes to mind as my first try at it.

As I began my leadership experience, Servant Leadership was a game I played rather than a strategy, but it became a custom and a philosophy when I realized the impact on the men. There were many times in the course of operations that this bond paid off. "Washing their feet" created a strong relationship that served us well.

Becoming a mentor is like being a Servant Leader...

The lessons of leadership I learned in the Navy were building blocks that I have added to during my career. My shipboard mentor was a former chief machinist who received his commission after serving in WWII as an enlisted sailor. He became the Chief of the Boat (COB) in submarines, and after the War received a commission as an officer and was now second in charge in the Engineering Department in Roosevelt. He was soft-spoken, but extremely competent.

Lieutenant Westbury did not have to take me under his wing, but he did, much to my benefit. We toured the engineering spaces (sometimes referred to as the bowels of the ship) when we had in-port duty together. We traced piping systems and discussed disaster procedures in detail—not just by talking about them, but by seeing where and how the action would take place if we ever did have to apply the shaft brake, or what would flood if got hit by a bomb or we took a torpedo. Westbury made sure I knew how to perform in emergent situations. When it came time for me to go before the qualifications review board so I could serve as the Officer of the Watch (be in charge of these four huge engines while we were at sea), I was ready, and had no problem passing both the oral and written exams.

The training and mentoring he gave was not something he had to do. I was being coached by a pro. He gave me very practical information, showed me lots of hidden places that could flood for various reasons and places where sailors could hide to sleep on a mid-watch, or to gamble or drink (which sometimes happened). I used the knowledge frequently and still wonder why West (as we affectionately called him) chose to mentor me in this way. He most likely saw some potential that made him want to invest in my future within the structure of the Engineering Department of the ship and in my Navy career. As a result of this bond, he and I were able to accomplish some really tough jobs during my tour in Roosevelt, including taking that huge vessel in and out of dry dock to get a new propeller, which was an engineering marvel. As a result of his work with me, leading and mentoring people became my style, which was "given" to me by Willie Westbury early in my career.

Educators should be Servant Leaders too...

I practiced the Servant Leadership philosophy during my twelve-year teaching career too. I found that young people also responded to the concept. When they saw me working at helping them learn, they in turn put forth their best effort on the lessons that I asked them to master. Being fourteen and learning the periodic table of the elements do not always go together. This is especially true if you are a female and because of your culture see no chance of ever needing this information.

I stressed the balance and order of the universe that allowed these elements to interact with each other in such a way as to permit us to understand them and benefit from that knowledge. The chemical bonding lessons and the calculations of molecular weight were so foreign to some of my students that they struggled for their meaning. Others, of course, saw the benefit of learning the building blocks of science so that as they progressed they were ready for more information that someday would permit them to go to college and learn some very specific, scientific disciplines. I am convinced that some of those young people learned those esoteric (to them) scientific principles simply because I asked them to. My guess is that they tried to please me because I was honest and fair with them and treated them with respect. I took them under my wing, and like Willie Westbury had done for me, showed them things that they should know but might not have learned any other way.

Spaghetti, anyone?

One of my strategies was to invite twelve students to our home each year for supper with my family. We accomplished this by use of a lottery. If they were selected, students got the chance to eat spaghetti that my wife had so lovingly prepared.

The "lucky" students were divided into two groups, six at a time. We drew only twelve names, since I could not serve all 135 students, and to pick only those I considered the very best for academic reasons might rule out those who needed to see another way of living in a family atmosphere. They had to agree to have their name thrown in the hat to begin with. After that, it was simply the luck of the draw.

At the event we played basketball in the driveway or softball in the backyard, whatever was the most appropriate for the time of year. Then, after about 45 minutes, we would gather around our big dining room table and eat spaghetti. I waited on them at the table and they put their very best manners on display, of that I am sure.

After the meal we talked about ourselves to get to know each other in a way not connected to school. We followed the meal by making a freezer of ice cream. The act of "turning" a freezer of homemade ice cream was always special to me when I was growing up. It was a bonding experience during the process and always ended up with some good eating. After all the fun, parents would show up to take their son or daughter home. It was all very simple.

Over the years I received many positive comments from now-grown adults who had the "Dinner with Lutz" experience. They loved it. They learned so much, not about facts, but about how to get people to work together, they said. I learned that the only way to reach some people that are put under your charge is to take time out and put them in a different setting (usually including food) to get them on a positive (productive) track.

Good leaders show compassion and love to their charges in ways that are appropriate for the situation so they can forge strong bonds. I consider it part of the Servant Leadership model. It is very simple, but it is often overlooked.

WWJD...What would John do?

Another example of Servant Leadership occurred much later in my career. We were in a strike situation in 1990. I was the Labor Relations Manager and deeply involved in negotiations. During the strike, we negotiated every other day for thirteen days before we reached an agreement with our union. During the off days when we were not negotiating, the management negotiating team worked in the plant like the rest of the salaried employees.

My job was to run the Surf-Perf machine. Surf and Perf were short for Surfaire and Perfaire, products that are found in the ceilings of doctor's offices and restaurants. They are supply or exhaust vents for air handling systems. The Surf-Perf machine joined the face to the back plate, which was covered by a blanket of fiberglass insulation.

The first step was to put a 2'x2' piece of stamped metal—called a face—in the jig and make sure it was secure. Next, a back plate, which was dome shaped, was placed on the inside of the face, then glue was sprayed on the back plate. A fiberglass blanket the shape of the back covered the glue. The machine crimped the edges together to make a solid unit. The machine would then move the assembly through a plastic wrapping process and out the other end to be put in a carton by a boxer—in this case, our vice president of marketing.

Our acting supervisor was the young engineer whose normal job was to improve the process by coordinating ideas from the operators and keep this machine running. He was the only one among this group of "scabs" who really understood the machine. We listened closely when John told us to do something. Once we got the hang of it, it went well, even though it was highly repetitive and very tiring.

John was our leader and would check how our supplies were holding out. If we got low on something, he would see to it that a service person would have what we needed there just in time. John checked the product for quality and he relieved us to get drinks and go to the bathroom. John was everywhere. He was the junior person in this operation in age and on the organizational chart, but we did what he said and he took care of our needs. We grew to respect John in a few short hours. John was giving the VP and me a lesson in Servant Leadership.

Since that time, whenever I was leader of a group, I made sure that I met with them, talked to them and found out what would make their jobs easier. I stood in for them if they were gone; I made sure we budgeted for their needs to be sure materials came in for the team to keep working on its tasks. I was their leader, but I did not simply delegate to them; I did whatever I could to be sure they could meet their goals in our effort to be successful.

The job of the Servant Leader was to remove the roadblocks that kept the team from accomplishing its mission. Each time some type of crisis came up that was impeding the team, I would think back to the

Surf-Perf machine and ask myself, "What would John do?" John was my hero and my role model when it came to Servant Leadership.

Analyze, Delegate, Supervise, Check, but also lead...

While being a Servant Leader sounds simple, it is hard work. I once was told by an older gentleman who had been a sales manager much of his life that his definition of leadership was found in four words: Analyze, Delegate, Supervise, Check. While this works as the old model, it leaves out the internal or operational definition of some of those terms, for within those four words lies the success or failure of the leader. How you analyze, delegate, supervise and check is as important as the fact that you accomplished all four pieces of the whole package. Leadership makes all the difference.

Analysis and delegation are self-explanatory. You consider the situation and delegate it to the right people to get it done. Supervise, however, is where there is a gap. How the supervisory process is carried out will determine the success or failure of the project. It is within the process of supervision that the leadership part and the people part come together. If the people are working like a team, free from as many external problems as possible, they will produce wonderfully. Remember the example of Captain Miller, my first Skipper? "A good ship is a happy ship." In this case, *good* is being efficient and productive. And *happy*, I think, means free from as many external pressures as can be managed.

When it comes to the last step, check, I am always amazed that this usually focuses on the negative. The term accountability creeps back into the discussion. Just as frequently, however, the check step might also signal a celebration.

If you have not experimented with Servant Leadership, you should. It will distinguish you as an informed leader.

6

Resolving Disputes

In *Leadership is an Art,* Max DePree writes that the first responsibility of a leader is to define reality. Mr. DePree, the long time CEO of the office furniture giant Herman Miller (one of the companies consistently on the 100 best employers in America) continues by saying that the last responsibility of leadership is to say "thank you."

A discussion about leadership would not be complete without addressing the issue of defining reality. So far, we have discussed reality in terms of performance counseling and getting work done with people, but there is an entirely different genre of leadership opportunities when we step into the area of resolving employee conflict. Being able to be humble and say thank you completes the cycle.

Conflict between two employees or among several employees in a work group is a time drain on any organization. The cost of conflict is addressed by Dan Dana, PhD, in his book *Managing Differences*. Dana (whose work can be seen on line at www.meadiationworks.com) lists eight cost factors in estimating what disputes costs an organization. The list includes:

1. Wasted time…which includes wages and benefit costs of both those who are in conflict and those who are not just casual observers of the battle.

2. Reduced decision quality by leaders or those affected by the conflict.

3. Loss (people simply quit rather than continue to work in a conflict-laden work culture) of skilled employees in terms of their wages and benefits.

4. Restructuring costs incurred by redesigning work around those in conflict.

5. Sabotage, theft, and damage.

6. Lowered job motivation in terms of reduced performance.

7. Lost work time incurred when one of those in conflict simply calls in sick and stays home.

8. Health costs to accommodate stress-related costs and health care premiums that are linked to rate of claims.

The costs get large very quickly when those eight factors are all added together. Dana's thesis is that the leaders can control those costs if they know how to skillfully manage conflict. Managing disputes between workers is a core competency of any leader and must be undertaken proactively.

My assumptions, while arrived at anecdotally, are validated by the successes I have had within the area of conflict management. They are based on Dana's conflict resolution model:

• Eighty percent of all disputes that take place within the workplace can be resolved by a skilled and empowered leader.

• People in conflict can negotiate an agreement between themselves if the leader intervenes and acts within a mediation model. In other words, acts impartially rather than from a posture of discipline.

• Workplace mediation does not require a professional to be successful.

Effectively resolving employee disputes is expected of leaders...

When the leader steps forward and confronts the conflict and resolves it, they have enhanced there stature not only with those in conflict, but also with those even remotely affected by the conflict within the organization. The caveat is that the leader must step up and get it done. In this case, they must dare to confront and dare to mediate.

Dana describes the essential process of mediating conflict as getting the disputants together face-to-face and allowing them to talk about the problem, without interruption, as long as it takes until they get resolution.

Intuitively, leaders know this, but they tend not to take this direct approach because most are conflict-averse. We, as humans, frequently exhaust every other method of solving the problem before we actually confront the two who are locked in this destructive behavior and get them to negotiate a settlement.

Organizations have permitted managers to enact some very creative workflow changes to keep from confronting the disputants. People are transferred, new processes are designed around the adversaries, and associates may quit their jobs just to avoid a confrontation. This is a business problem. It is also a leadership problem.

The leader must define reality by discussing the issue with each party and then get them together to talk about it as long as it takes to come to a new reality. It sounds logical enough, but dealing with conflict head-on makes most of us squirm. Leaders know this has to be done, but they avoid the problem either because they are not sure enough of themselves and their skills or they have ignored the pain and left the conflict unchecked.

One manager I knew was aware that the conflict between the two parties must be resolved, so he gave the responsibility to resolve it back to them. "You two resolve this thing in the next couple of days or I will resolve it for you, and you may not like my resolution," he told them.

(Sounds like an idle threat to me.) Another manager threatened discipline for one or both disputants if they did not self-resolve their differences. (Again, leadership has given way to intimidation.)

I can only conclude that the two leaders took their respective approaches because they did not know how to manage the process or they were so conflict-averse they were afraid to sit down with the two and help them come to some common ground and come up with a both-gain solution.

Using the Dana model, the skillful leader will:

1. Interview each employee alone and determine their readiness to use mediation.

2. Assure each that this is not a disciplinary meeting and that mediation, unlike arbitration will not declare one the winner.

3. Frame the dispute in business terms, which means that the leader has jurisdiction in the dispute, no matter what the original source of the dispute, since it is now impeding their performance and adversely affecting the organization.

4. Get the two parties in the same room to talk it out without interruption for as long as it takes.

5. Write an agreement and have each person sign it.

Dana says that in this model, the leader/mediator has three responsibilities: (1) Keep them talking (what he calls the Essential Process), (2) Support conciliatory gestures, and (3) Wait. According to Dana, it does not take mediation skills to accomplish a "breakthrough." What is necessary is to allow the natural forces to weave their magic.

Effective leaders know that putting this problem to rest quickly is in the best interest of all: the individuals in conflict, those around them, the organization and certainly for the leader.

Dispute resolution is a key ingredient to increasing the stature of the leader in the eyes of subordinates. To permit a disagreement to go on and on is a sure sign of a weak and ineffective leader. Sorry, there is no other observation to make. Employees surrounded by strife will not work effectively, productively or harmoniously until the problem is resolved.

DePree's observation about the leader's first responsibility, which is to define reality, is right on target. The reality in a dispute is that it sucks the time and energy right out of the organization for as long as it festers. Reality is that the rift needs to be fixed. Reality is that the leader is not leading until they take the initiative to solve the problem and put it to rest.

Dana's model can be learned in about six hours with a trained instructor. It then requires practice so that the leader is comfortable with the process and is able to recognize the signals that a resolution is possible. It is worth trying. I have used it many times and it really works.

The ability to effectively resolve conflict is the mark of a leader. It also sends a message to the other associates: we work for someone who *Dares to Lead.*

Conclusion

If you ever served in a leadership role, you realize that being an effective leader is hard work. If a leader has charisma, it helps, but as one astute observer said, "The downside of charisma is arrogance." If you think you have some charismatic traits, consider it a gift, but don't flaunt it, since you may come across as arrogant and uppity to your charges. Those characteristics become a dulling force for any leader. You are much better off to be perceived as being "of the people" rather than above them.

We all do not have magnetic personalities that allow us to be, as Malcolm Gladwell in his book *The Tipping Point* identifies, connectors. Gladwell describes connectors as "those among us who know lots of people, and in turn are people to whom others come with information." Connectors make things happen because of the efficiency with which they communicate. Leaders need to be more like connectors, even if they are not hardwired that way. It is a trait that can be cultivated within the workplace and practiced eight (or ten) hours a day. That is what building work relationships is all about. Having effective relationships with those being led is the essence of leadership.

DARE TO LEAD ALL LEVELS...

The manufacturing CEO who builds relationships with the maintenance department's key employees will become well connected and in the know. The school administrator who can talk openly to the custodial staff will rapidly be able to take the pulse of the school. The hospital chief administrator who is visible and approachable to the employees in hospitality services and those with direct patient care who change the beds or wash the linens will be able to make a much faster and accurate read as to the effectiveness of the organization. The employee relations manager who builds relationships within the rank and file, not just with the union leadership, will be a better problem solver and gain credibility and respect when the hard decisions have to be made. The supervisor who "touches" all his people several times a shift and then thanks them for their good work at the end of the day will be sought out when problems begin to arise, and therefore are more easily managed.

Effective leadership is being able to put on your "actor clothes" and your "work mask" every day and be fully involved with those you lead, even if you don't feel like it. If the leader is consistent, their style will not be perceived as acting. It will not come across as fake or phony; it will be seen as sincere and genuine. Being a good leader often takes you out of your comfort zone. It requires you to be upbeat most of the time, especially when you don't feel like it, and it demands that you hold firm to your principles.

DARE TO LEAD IN ALL TYPES OF ENTERPRISES...

Successful teachers have learned these lessons and proven them over and over during their tenure in the classroom. If the educational leader uses the relational side of their pedagogical skills effectively, they build a wellspring of good feeling which quickly translates to good learning. That is why testing the subject knowledge of a teacher is not always a good indicator of their effectiveness. I have found that there is little difference between the classroom and the office or factory when it comes to cultivating mutual respect.

Captain Miller, skipper of the Roosevelt, used the ship's loud-speaker system (1MC) several times a week to address the crew. "This is your happy captain speaking," he would frequently begin. "We have some difficult operations scheduled for the next several days and it is going to require the best that each of you has to offer," he might go on to say. Being positive and creating a Happy Ship attitude among the mostly teenage crew was essential in selling a life that meant long hours of work and sacrifice by being away from family for months at a time. But do you know what? It worked. It was the captain in the movie *Mr. Roberts* in reverse. Miller got those young men to perform in a manner that earned the FDR recognition for safety and operational readiness while he was the commanding officer.

DARE TO BE A SERVANT LEADER...

Being able to touch the souls of the people the leader is assigned to supervise is possible by practicing the art of Servant Leadership. Removing roadblocks, or at least being willing to work to try to remove roadblocks so they can accomplish their best work makes the servant leader more effective, especially during challenging times. Working for consistency and fairness in each decision supports the leader as being worthy of having the trust of the people given to them to lead.

A good leader will never take the goodwill of their people for granted. If you think you have done enough over time and now deserve their respect, then you are asking your charges to withdraw more from the relationship bank than you have put in. There will be an overdraft charge. Always carry a good balance in that account. When times get really rough—and there will be tough times—you will need all the goodwill that is available in your relationship bank account. You should plan to have more deposits in that bank than there will be with-drawals against the account.

DARE TO LEAD...

Make your expectations known. As the supervisory model states: analyze, delegate, supervise, check. And by all means, be ready to confront
poor performance. Be a coach. Point out how the play could have been
run better, and congratulate the team when they do well. This model
works in holding the team members accountable to their own higher
standards (by taking ownership) without ever using the word "accountable."

Find a mentor. Look for someone whom you can trust and with
whom you can discuss the tough issues that will inevitably come up.
But choose wisely. Don't invest your career in someone who does not
have the track record that deserves your trust. Then, when the time
comes, by all means, be a mentor. Give back tenfold what you have
received. You'll feel much better for it.

That's it. Now, go forth and Dare to Lead.

Acknowledgements

The giants who guided me during my career were unaware that they would be mentioned in a book, of that I am sure. They performed the way they did for purely personal reasons. They were either reciprocating behavior that was given to them during their careers or they clearly saw the need to mentor a neophyte. Either way, I became the benefactor of their gifts and experience. I am grateful. Without their guidance, I would have become a member of the floundering masses—part of the great unwashed, so to speak.

There were those along the way who pointed me in the wrong direction as well. They unknowingly gave me examples of leadership styles not to emulate. They too were unaware that they were giving me examples for a book on leadership, albeit bad ones. But it is well that they gave them to me so I could contrast their trashy styles with the good stuff I learned. By setting poor examples, they helped me more clearly define the right way to lead.

We have choices throughout life, and a choice that I made was to follow those who cultivated a close knit (what we refer to today as a team) atmosphere. I left organizations that were headed in the wrong direction, in my estimation. Those that I migrated to were much more relational in style. I was comfortable working for them. Those organizations showed great synergy, and they were successful by any measure.

I will mention a few individuals here because they stand out. They are not the only people I learned from, but they are significant and should be acknowledged. They include:

- **Raymond C. Lutz**, DDS, Lt. Col. U.S. Army Reserve (Retired)—my father. Dad, a dentist, was called to active duty in both WWI and WWII. He stayed in the reserves after WWI and thus was activated at the age of 47 shortly after Pearl Harbor. I was an infant when he was called up in 1942. When I was a teenager, Dad gave me my first glimpse of the term Christian World View. He died when I was 20, leaving me with many unanswered questions about life. He was a leader who held you to your word, but was a compassionate, gentle man.

- **Dorothy Lutz**, my mother. The War caused her to be a single parent mom for almost four years. She elected to move her young family to the country while dad was gone, thus we became farmers. This was in the day of limited indoor plumbing, horse-drawn farm implements and coal fired furnaces. She taught the lessons of leadership based on Christianity and Biblical truths, snippets of which were written on a chalkboard in the kitchen as a reminder to all of us.

- **Joseph, David, James Lutz and Phyllis Lutz Williams**; my siblings. There was every reason to believe I would be spoiled, since I was the last child in a relatively large family, but as siblings do, they all kept me on the straight and narrow. They demanded excellence in my work as I grew up on the farm. I learned from each of them, but the underlying message was to respect others. Joe, the oldest, was HR Director for a division of Cargill and we had delightful discussions about leadership. Dave, the preacher, is still leading a flock and exhorting the Word. Those two were surrogate fathers to me at various times and from them I learned much. Phyllis and Jim are retired teachers. I especially got to watch Jim at his craft during the 1970s and part of the 1980s while I too was in the classroom. Jim was a master teacher/leader. Phyllis' influence was limited to my early years. She gave me a love for baseball. We listened endlessly to our dear Pirates on KDKA.

- **Harold D. Green**. H.D. was Brother Dave's father-in-law who owned an 80 cow dairy operation in Western Pennsylvania. I worked for him during three summers while I was in high school in the late 1950s. He was a tough taskmaster. His two oldest sons were decorated Marine combat veterans in the

Pacific Theater of WWII. They were tough because they were raised that way; HD was tough. By the time I came along, he was over 60 and much mellower. He had patience to guide me in the lessons of the care and management of farm equipment and the herd of dairy cows. What could have been a terrible relationship was one that allowed me to grow. I have often thought of his patience with me when I would grow impatient with others.

- **Vice Admiral Jerry Miller,** USN (Retired). Captain (then) Miller was my first commanding officer. He was skipper of the USS Franklin D. Roosevelt (CVA 42) when I joined the crew in the fall of 1963. At the time, Captain Miller was a 45-year-old Naval Academy graduate, WWII, Korea and Cold War veteran. He served in surface combatants during the War and later became a naval aviator. He commanded aircraft squadrons in Korea, skippered an ammunition supply ship and a carrier before he was promoted to Rear Admiral, then Vice Admiral and became Commander of the Second Fleet (US East Coast) and the Sixth Fleet (Mediterranean Sea), retiring after a distin-guished career in 1974. In the fall of 2003 I had the privilege of reacquainting with him through his publisher via e-mail after he authored an article in a magazine I read. We have been able to exchange thoughts on leadership, which he distilled into a very brief definition: "Treat people with respect and use common sense."

- **Lieutenant Willie Westbury,** USN (Retired). West was the Main Propulsion Assistant in FDR and initially my boss's boss. He became my mentor and later my boss when I was promoted to Boiler Division Officer. He taught me the value of training and accountability. Ex-enlisted officers typically did not like to work with we OCS types. We were college graduates and for the most part they were not. We knew nothing about the navy and they knew much. We were in our early twenties, and they were ten to twenty years older at a similar rank. We were eligible for command at sea and most of them not. Many of them at that time were WWII combat veterans and we were green. "West" took me under his wing and put up with my questions and observations. His coolness and confidence under stress along with his patience were valuable lessons.

- **Jerome Galvin**. Jerry was my first boss at Campbell Soup. He was a dynamo and did everything he could to expose me to the hierarchy at CSC. His mantra was, "There is an easy way and a hard way to do everything. Let's find the easy way." This comment was made in the context of gaining the cooperation of others to support a program or initiative. Jerry was a safety expert out of the DuPont organization. He gave me a crash course in big company politics (relationships) which at the same time soured and fascinated me.

- **Frank G. Moore**. While Frank is somewhat older than I, he was a peer at Campbell Soup Company when I worked at the corporate office…he as safety manager and I as corporate training manager. Frank is African-American and coached me on race through the inflammatory climate of the late 1960s. Camden, NJ was burning and National Guard troops manned the overpasses on the highways I took to work following Dr. Martin Luther King's assassination. A native of Philadelphia, Frank gave this rural lad accurate information on black culture and thought that served me well over the years. His mentoring is directly responsible for my close affiliation today with the Woodrick Institute for the Study of Racism and Diversity located in Grand Rapids, MI and headed by Dr. Steve Robbins.

- **Samuel F. Morehead**. Coach Morehead was the middle school principal where I taught. A WWII combat veteran, he parlayed his GI Bill education in teaching of mathematics into a career as teacher, administrator, football coach (life's a cinch by the inch, but hard by the yard), and basketball coach (Hustle and Harmony was his motto). Sam is an example of a Servant Leader and a dynamic person.

- **Lawrence B. Lee.** Larry is a contemporary of mine and was a very experienced and capable CEO of Hart & Cooley, Inc. for over 14 years. Larry overlooked my 13-year absence from industry while teaching and permitted me to be hired back into the HR profession. I was not a direct report, but we talked often and problem solved within and outside the corporate structure. He sent me to the University of Michigan to brush up on union contract administration and to Cornell University to learn about change management within an organization. He gave me carte blanche to develop our total quality management (TQM) initiative and to implement it. He later appointed me integration manager of an acquisition of a fan business when we took over ownership. I frequently joke that I attended the L. B. Lee graduate school of human resources. He was a great mentor. Under Larry's leadership we developed the Core Values of our company, which guided the way we managed the business for a number of years. He is a Christian gentleman and gifted leader.

- **Judeth Tamar Newham**, RN, President/CEO of Holland Community Hospital from 1991-2002. Judy welcomed me as a board member in 1994 and tutored me during my year as Board Chair in 1998 through some very touchy situations. She sent me to Harvard Business School for a week to learn how to be a board chair of a non-profit organization. There I rubbed elbows with leaders on a national level. When I joined the HCH staff I resigned from the board and became a worker bee in the hospital leading the HR staff for three years.

There were other leaders who influenced me incrementally and I am grateful to them all. The ones mentioned above were singled out because each gave me one or more epiphanies while under their leadership. Where did I learn the most? Without question my 55 months in the Navy had a great impact in my development initially. I had my eyes opened to the corporate world at Campbell Soup and then was able to practice my leadership style in the classroom for over 12 years as a middle school teacher. But my 14 plus years with Hart & Cooley (in the metal stamping business) were the most significant. I worked in that environment the longest and was part of the management team that worked to establish a climate like the Big Dogs in our community: Herman Miller, Donnelly Corp., Haworth, Johnson Controls, and others devoted to a participative management approach. We proved that we could take a union environment and culture and raise it a level or two to become known as a good place to work. That was very gratifying.

Bibliography

Dana, Dan *Managing Differences;* Third Edition, MTI Publications, 1988, 2001

Davis, Bart O. *Restoring Dignity & Leadership;* Griffiths, 1999

DePree, Max *Leadership is an Art;* Doubleday, 1989

Elgin, Suzette *Success with the Gentle Art of Verbal Self Defense;* Prentice Hall, 1989

Gladwell, Malcolm *The Tipping Point;* Little Brown, 2000

Jones, Laurie Beth *Jesus, CEO;* Hyperion, 1995

0-595-30901-1

Printed in the United States
18537LVS00004B/1-102

9 780595 309016